641.8   Ashley, Susan.
Ash   I can make a sandwich

=

MAY 2 9		
APR. 1 2		
OCT 2 6 2012		
FEB 1 9 2013		
NOV ? 1 2013		
JAN - 6 2014		
JAN 2 8 2014		
NOV 1 7 2014		
FEB 2 0 2015		
MAY 8 2018		
NOV 9		

Demco, Inc. 38-293

F&P - E

AR 1.1
0.5 pB

I CAN
DO IT!

I CAN MAKE
A SANDWICH

by Susan Ashley

Photographs by Gregg Andersen

Reading consultant: Susan Nations, M.Ed., author/literacy coach/consultant

WEEKLY WR READER®
EARLY LEARNING LIBRARY

Please visit our web site at: **www.earlyliteracy.cc**
For a free color catalog describing Weekly Reader® Early Learning Library's
list of high-quality books, call 1-877-445-5824 (USA) or 1-800-387-3178 (Canada).
Weekly Reader® Early Learning Library's fax: (414) 336-0164.

Library of Congress Cataloging-in-Publication Data

Ashley, Susan.
  I can make a sandwich / by Susan Ashley.
    p. cm. — (I can do it!)
  Includes bibliographical references and index.
  ISBN 0-8368-4323-1 (lib. bdg.)
  ISBN 0-8368-4330-4 (softcover)
  1. Sandwiches—Juvenile literature. I. Title. II. I can do it! (Milwaukee, Wis.)
  TX818.A84   2004
  641.8'4—dc22   2004045128

This edition first published in 2005 by
Weekly Reader® Early Learning Library
330 West Olive Street, Suite 100
Milwaukee, WI 53212 USA

Copyright © 2005 by Weekly Reader® Early Learning Library

Editor: JoAnn Early Macken
Graphic Designer: Melissa Valuch
Art Director: Tammy West
Picture Researcher: Diane Laska-Swanke
Photographer: Gregg Andersen

Printed in the United States of America

1 2 3 4 5 6 7 8 9 08 07 06 05 04

Note to Educators and Parents

Reading is such an exciting adventure for young children! They are beginning to integrate their oral language skills with written language. To encourage children along the path to early literacy, books must be colorful, engaging, and interesting; they should invite the young reader to explore both the print and the pictures.

I Can Do It! is a new series designed to help young readers learn how ordinary children reach everyday goals. Each book describes a different task that any child can be proud to accomplish.

Each book is specially designed to support the young reader in the reading process. The familiar topics are appealing to young children and invite them to read — and re-read — again and again. The full-color photographs and enhanced text further support the student during the reading process.

In addition to serving as wonderful picture books in schools, libraries, homes, and other places where children learn to love reading, these books are specifically intended to be read within an instructional guided reading group. This small group setting allows beginning readers to work with a fluent adult model as they make meaning from the text. After children develop fluency with the text and content, the book can be read independently. Children and adults alike will find these books supportive, engaging, and fun!

— Susan Nations, M.Ed., author, literacy coach, and consultant in literacy development

I can make a sandwich. I can make a peanut butter and jelly sandwich.

First, I find the things
I need. I ask my
mother to help me.

I need five things —
- bread
- peanut butter
- jelly
- a blunt knife
- a plate

I take out two slices
of bread.

I spread peanut butter on one slice of bread.

I spread jelly on the other slice of bread.

I put the two slices together. I put my sandwich on a plate. I cut it in half.

Am I done? Not yet!
I must clean up. I put
everything away.

Now I can eat. Yum!

Glossary

blunt — not sharp

slices — thin pieces

spread — to put on in a smooth motion

For More Information

Books

Kids Cook! Fabulous Food for the Whole Family. Sarah Williamson, Zachary Williamson, and Lorette Trezzo-Braren (Williamson Publishing)

Kids in the Kitchen: The Library of Multicultural Cooking (series). (PowerKids Press)

Let's Read About Food (series). Cynthia Fitterer Klingel (Weekly Reader Early Learning Library)

Where Does Our Food Come From? (series). Gretchen Will Mayo (Weekly Reader Early Learning Library)

Web Sites

Botham Bakery's Guide to Bread: From Seed to Sandwich

www.botham.co.uk/seed/first.htm
A fun history of bread

Index

About the Author

Susan Ashley has written more than twenty-five books for children. She has lived all over the United States and in Europe. Thanks to her travels, she has become very good at reading maps and writing letters. She also likes making — and eating — sandwiches. Susan lives in Wisconsin with her husband and two cats. The cats like it when she makes tuna sandwiches!